BBC
DOCTOR WHO
Mummy on the Orient Express

A story based on the original script by
JAMIE MATHIESON

Level 3

Retold by Jane Rollason

Series Editors: Andy Hopkins and Jocelyn Potter

T0352427

Pearson Education Limited

KAO Two

KAO Park, Harlow,

Essex, CM17 9NA, England

and Associated Companies throughout the world.

ISBN: 978-1-292-20583-0

This edition first published by Pearson Education Ltd 2018

5 7 9 10 8 6

BBC

BBC, DOCTOR WHO (word marks, logos and devices), TARDIS, DALEKS, CYBERMAN
and K-9 (word marks and devices) are trade marks of the British Broadcasting
Corporation and are used under licence. BBC logo © BBC 1996. Doctor Who logo © BBC
2009. Licensed by BBC Worldwide Limited.

The authors have asserted their moral rights in accordance
with the Copyright Designs and Patents Act 1988
Set in 9pt/14pt Xenois Slab Pro
SWTC/05

Published by Pearson Education Limited

For a complete list of the titles available in the Pearson English Readers series, visit
www.pearsonenglishreaders.com.
Alternatively, write to your local Pearson Education office or
to Pearson English Readers Marketing Department,
Pearson Education, KAO Two, KAO Park, Harlow, Essex, CM17 9NA

Contents

In this story

The Doctor

The Doctor is an alien, a Time Lord from the planet Gallifrey. Everyone calls him 'the Doctor'. He travels the universe, has adventures and saves people in danger. He has two hearts, and he is about 2,000 years old.

When the Doctor's body becomes old or ill, he changes it for a new one. He has had many different bodies before the one in this story.

The Doctor doesn't use a gun, and tries not to kill anyone. His sonic screwdriver has many uses. It can unlock doors, use technology and see inside things. He also has a plain white card in a card holder. He shows it when he needs to. The reader sees on it what the Doctor wants him or her to see.

The TARDIS

The Doctor travels through time and space in a time machine called the TARDIS. On the outside, the TARDIS looks like a blue police box from Earth. These blue boxes were used in the UK, many years ago, to call the police. The inside is very different. It is a high-tech spaceship, much bigger than on the outside.

The Doctor's Companion: Clara Oswald

The Doctor usually travels with someone from Earth. In this story, the Doctor's companion is Clara Oswald, an English teacher at a London school. As a companion, she is the Doctor's assistant and friend, and she helps him on his adventures. At the end of an adventure, the TARDIS returns the companion to Earth. They usually arrive back at exactly the same time as they left.

The Foretold

The Foretold is a mummy, and is thousands of years old.

Captain Quell

Captain Quell is the captain of a train called the Orient Express.

Gus

The computer on the Orient Express is called Gus. He has a very friendly voice – but is he really friendly?

Perkins

Perkins is the chief engineer on the Orient Express.

Maisie Pitt

Maisie Pitt is a passenger on the Orient Express. She has had a difficult life.

Introduction

The mummy was in front of him. Its ugly mouth was open and its hands came towards him. He felt them pressing on his head.

When the Doctor and his companion Clara Oswald arrive on the Orient Express, Clara is very excited. She thinks they are taking a short holiday. The Orient Express is the world's most famous train, and this one is travelling through space! But there is an alien on the train and it has already killed one of the passengers. Can the Doctor and Clara solve the mystery of the mummy? What does it want? How does it choose who to kill? Why can only the victim see it?

The mummy joins a long line of aliens that the Doctor has tried to stop. *Doctor Who* first appeared on television in 1963 in black and white, and it was the first science fiction programme for children in the UK. It was a great success, with its new electronic sounds and crazy stories in outer space. The programmes were shown until 1989. Sixteen years later, *Doctor Who* returned with a new writing team. The stories became funnier, and more adult, but the central idea is the same. The Doctor travels through space in the TARDIS, his time machine, fighting aliens. Since 1963, the BBC has made more than 800 *Doctor Who* programmes. Today they are shown in many countries around the world.

Peter Capaldi played the Twelfth Doctor. The Doctor always has the same history, but each actor brings something new to the part. Capaldi has always loved *Doctor Who*. When he went into the TARDIS for the first time, he felt at home. 'I know how to work the TARDIS,' he said. 'I've known for a long time!'

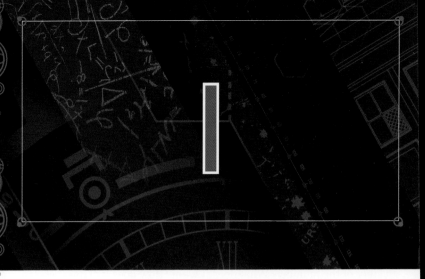

The Mummy

Nobody noticed when the lights went dim for a second.

'Start the clock,' said a voice, but nobody heard. The clock started counting. 66 seconds, 65, 64 ...

A train was travelling at high speed. But this was no ordinary train. It was travelling through space, and it was the Orient Express, the King of Trains. Many years ago, the Orient Express was Europe's favourite train, taking rich people from Paris to Istanbul. This wasn't the *real* Orient Express, of course, but it was a perfect copy.

Inside the train, the passengers were all in the dining carriage. They were enjoying a fine evening meal, expensive wine and a view of the stars, while they passed through the universe. It was a very special trip, calling at a different planet every few days. Everyone was dressed for dinner – dinner in 1925. The men wore black dinner suits and the women wore beautiful dresses.

A waitress walked between the tables, carrying bowls of soup. At one end of the dining car, an old lady sat in a wheelchair, opposite a much younger woman. Neither woman smiled when the waitress put down their soup. Then the old lady looked up, and suddenly her face changed.

... 50, 49, 48 ...

'Is there some sort of silly party this evening, Maisie?' she asked, looking towards the other end of the car in surprise.

'I don't think so,' said Maisie Pitt, the younger woman. 'Why do you ask, Mama?'

'Look at that person at the end of the dining car,' said the old lady. 'He's dressed as a mummy ...'

The mummy was very tall. It looked straight at her while it moved slowly down the car towards her. Dirty old bandages covered its body, with bits hanging from its arms and legs. It had black holes in place of eyes, and its mouth was full of broken teeth.

... 40, 39, 38 ...

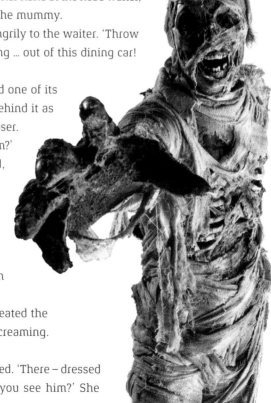

The old lady waved her hand at the head waiter, keeping her eyes on the mummy.

'You!' she called angrily to the waiter. 'Throw that ... man ... that thing ... out of this dining car! It's not amusing!'

The mummy pulled one of its feet along the floor behind it as it came closer and closer.

'*Which* man, madam?' the head waiter said, quietly and politely.

He looked along the empty space between the tables to the end of the car. He couldn't see a man or a mummy.

'*Which* man?!' repeated the old woman, almost screaming.

... 30, 29, 28 ...

'*That* man!' she cried. 'There – dressed as a mummy! Can't you see him?' She turned to the young woman. 'Maisie, tell him.'

The old lady wasn't angry now; she was afraid. Other passengers turned to look at her white face and frightened eyes.

'Mama!' said the younger woman, looking around. 'There's nobody there.'

... 20, 19, 18 ...

'Don't you lie to me, girl,' said the old lady. Then she shook her finger at the mummy. 'Stop it!' she cried. 'Stop it immediately!'

To the other passengers, she seemed to be shaking her finger at the empty air.

... 10, 9, 8 ...

The mummy was very close to the old lady now, but still only she could see it. It moved its ugly dead head towards her, with its broken teeth and bad smell. She tried to disappear into her wheelchair.

'You're not well, Mama,' said the younger woman. 'Shall I get your medicine? Would you like to go back to your room?'

'Get it off me!' cried the old lady.

... 3, 2, 1 ...

The mummy reached its hands out and pressed them hard against the old lady's head. She shut her eyes tight. And then she fell back into her seat and stopped moving.

... zero ...

The younger woman jumped up and screamed. The other passengers stood up too. They wanted to see what was happening.

'Is there a doctor on the train?' cried the young woman. 'We need a doctor!'

Further along the train, there was a sudden strange noise and a bright light. A blue police box arrived from nowhere. The door of the box opened and a man stepped out. He was followed by a young woman. They were dressed like the other passengers, in clothes from the 1920s.

The box wasn't a police box; it was the TARDIS. It was a machine that could travel through time and space. The man wasn't a man; he was a Time Lord from the planet Gallifrey. He was called the Doctor. The young woman really *was* a young woman, from Earth. Her name was Clara Oswald. Back on Earth, she was an English teacher, with a boyfriend called Danny Pink. Clara was also the Doctor's companion on his adventures in space.

'Our last journey together, Clara,' said the Doctor.

And this *was* the last of those adventures. Clara was angry with the Doctor, and she wanted to stay on Earth now with Danny. This trip was a surprise gift from the Doctor before they said goodbye.

She looked around, puzzled. This wasn't a beautiful planet full of strange aliens. It was a small, dark room full of suitcases.

'Er ... wonderful,' she said, not meaning it. 'But Doctor, where are we? Why has the TARDIS brought us here?'

'This carriage is for the suitcases,' said the Doctor. 'It's not very wonderful. But thank you for saying so!'

He took Clara to the door to the next carriage, and opened it.

'*This* is the wonderful part,' he said. 'Welcome to the Orient Express!'

The Sad Smile

The door opened into the train's bar, where guests were enjoying a drink after dinner. There was a singer, and some passengers were dancing. Others were sitting and talking, and watching the view of the universe through the train windows. Life continued as usual. The death of the old lady – well, that was sad, of course, but old ladies have to die some time. And this was a special holiday on a special train.

The Doctor and Clara stepped into the bar.

'It's almost exactly like the first Orient Express,' said the Doctor, 'but it's a little bigger and it's in space. And it doesn't really need its wheels. It's flying, as you can see …'

The Doctor was talking, but Clara didn't seem to be listening. He looked at her face. Was she smiling?

'You're doing it again,' he said.

'Doing what?' she asked.

'That smile,' said the Doctor. 'It's the *sad* smile. It's a smile, but you're sad. I don't understand it. It's two opposite feelings at the same time. I always think you're malfunctioning.'

'I'm sorry,' said Clara.

'I thought this was a good last journey for us …' said the Doctor.

There was a singer, and some passengers were dancing.

'Yes, it is,' said Clara. 'You've chosen a good one.'

She smiled again and took the Doctor's arm. They walked to a table and looked out at the stars.

'Dear guests,' said a voice. It was the train's computer. 'Please look through the windows on the right of the train. You can see the Magellan Black Hole*. Isn't it beautiful?'

'Oh, I remember when there were beautiful planets here,' said the Doctor. 'That big black hole has eaten them all now ...'

He looked at Clara. She wasn't listening.

'There's that smile again,' he said. 'How do you do that?'

*black hole: When a big star dies, its planets die too. A large black hole is left in space.

Clara laughed, but then her face grew serious.

'I really thought that I hated you,' she said.

'Well,' said the Doctor, 'thanks for not telling me that!' He turned back to the window and started to describe the lost planets. 'One of the planets here was called Obsidian. It was completely dark all the time ...'

Clara still wasn't listening.

'I hated you for weeks,' she told him.

'Fine,' said the Doctor. 'And the planet next to Obsidian ... it's made of trees. Only trees! Imagine that.'

Clara stopped him. She was remembering their last adventure. They were on the moon – the Earth's Moon. They discovered something very strange about it – the Moon was an egg! And then it started to break open. Inside was an alien life form. Clara and the Doctor sent a message to Earth: 'Shall we kill the alien or can it live? It's only a baby. But if it lives, perhaps it will attack the Earth. Or if the Moon dies, perhaps the Earth will die too.' Clara and the Doctor waited while people on Earth discussed the problem. And then their answer came back: 'Kill it!' But when Clara turned to the Doctor for help, he wasn't there. He simply disappeared and left her with the terrible decision.

The memory of that day on the Moon was very painful. It was the worst day of her life. She tried to explain her feelings to the Doctor.

'I went to see a singer one time,' she said. 'I can't remember his name. But do you know what he said?'

'Of course I don't know,' the Doctor answered. 'How *can* I know?'

'The singer said, "We only hate people that we love",' said Clara.

'That doesn't make sense,' said the Doctor.

'Hate's a strong feeling,' replied Clara. 'I hated you for some time, but only because you're so important to me. I was very unhappy about the Moon thing and the big decision. But of course I don't *really* hate you.' She looked sadly at the Doctor. 'I can't hate you. I just can't do this any more.'

The Doctor hoped that was the end of the discussion. He couldn't talk about human feelings. He didn't know what to say.

'Can I talk about the planets again now?' he asked.

'Yes,' laughed Clara. 'Tell me!'

'The planet Thedium 4 was here. It rained all the time, and it wasn't nice clean rain. It was dangerous rain. I went there once but I didn't stay long.'

'That's a lie,' said a voice loudly. 'You *didn't* go there.'

It was Maisie Pitt. She was standing near their table. Other guests turned to look at her. Just then the bar door opened, and the train's captain came in with his guards.

'I'm sorry?' said Clara, smiling at Maisie. 'Were you speaking to us?'

'He lied about Thedium 4,' said Maisie, pointing at the Doctor. 'It was destroyed thousands of years ago. He was never there. I study the history of black holes, so I know.'

The captain spoke to the young woman. 'Miss Pitt,' he said. 'Perhaps you would like to go back to your room?'

'That man's lying,' she said unhappily.

'My guard will go with you, Miss Pitt. This is a very difficult time for you.'

The guard and the young woman left the bar.

'I'm so sorry about that,' said the captain. 'But I think we can forgive her ... after her difficult day.' Then he looked more closely at them, puzzled. 'I don't believe we've met. I'm Captain Quell.'

'I'm Clara,' said Clara. 'And this is the Doctor.'

'Ah! Another one,' said Captain Quell.

'Another what?' asked Clara.

'Everyone on this trip seems to be a doctor or a professor of something,' replied Captain Quell. He turned to the Doctor. 'And what are you a doctor of?'

This was not an easy question for the Doctor to answer. What *was* he a doctor of?

'Aliens that live in human stomachs,' he said. It was the first idea that came into his head.

The captain looked at him through narrow eyes. He didn't believe him.

'Hm,' he said. 'Perhaps Miss Pitt was right about you.'

He turned to leave. Clara called to him.

'What's wrong with Miss Pitt?' she asked. '"A difficult time," you said. Has something happened?'

The captain looked puzzled.

'You mean you really don't know?' he said.

The Wheelchair

'So there's a body and there's a mummy,' said Clara to the Doctor, outside their rooms. She spoke quietly. It was late, and they were tired. 'Why can't we just have a ride on a train? Something always has to happen!'

'It's probably nothing,' replied the Doctor. 'Old ladies die all the time.'

'And the mummy?' said Clara.

'Well, she was the only person who saw it,' said the Doctor. 'So perhaps it wasn't really there. Maybe because she was dying, she imagined it. She *was* over a hundred years old ...'

'... says the 2,000-year-old man,' said Clara. 'But you think there's nothing to worry about. So that's fine with me!'

They still had their drinks with them. The Doctor held his glass in the air. 'To our last journey,' he said.

'Our last, yeah ...,' said Clara. She really wasn't happy about this. She loved travelling with the Doctor. Was she wrong to end it? 'But I *will* see you again, won't I? It's not really goodbye, is it?'

'Isn't it?' said the Doctor. 'Isn't that what *you* wanted?'

'Well, yes, but ... you'll come to *dinner* at my house, won't you?' She looked at the Doctor for a few seconds. 'No, you won't come to dinner,' she said. 'Time Lords don't come to dinner, do they?' She touched his glass with hers. 'To our last journey!'

The train continued its journey through space, on its way to the next planet stop.

The Doctor lay on his bed in his room. He was talking to himself.

'It's nothing,' said Doctor One. 'I'm almost sure it's nothing. It's just an old lady who imagines things. No mummy. No problem to solve.'

'"*Almost*",' repeated Doctor Two. 'So you're not sure?'

'OK,' replied Doctor One, 'let's say "probably".'

'Well, that's a big drop. That's a drop from "yes" to "maybe",' said Doctor Two.

In the next room, Clara was lying on her bed and talking on the phone to her boyfriend. Clara and Danny taught at the same school. In fact, that was where they met. Danny knew all about Clara's trips with the Doctor. He also knew that the universe was full of aliens. But he often worried about Clara and her dangerous adventures. When Clara told him the story of the alien and the Moon, he was *really* unhappy. The Doctor sometimes pushed her too far. Before he became a teacher, Danny was a soldier. His officer was similar to the Doctor; he also pushed Danny too far.

But now, Danny wasn't worrying.

'A train in space?' he said. 'That sounds great.'

'So what are you saying? You think it's OK to spend time with him in space. Are you forgetting the Moon thing?'

Danny was lying on the sofa at home in another world.

'I know he left you alone on the Moon ... But you still like him ... as a friend, of course. You should just enjoy your space train. It's not dangerous, is it?'

'No – you're right,' said Clara. 'This isn't dangerous – or very exciting. It's nice, but it's quite boring really.'

They said goodbye, and Clara tried to sleep.

The Doctor was still discussing the mummy with himself. He was walking up and down in his little room.

'You know what this sounds like?' said Doctor Two.

'No, do tell me,' answered Doctor One.

'A mummy that only the victim can see,' said Doctor Two.

'You're right,' answered Doctor One.

The Doctor picked up his coat and left his room. He was smiling. He had a mystery to solve. He was happy.

He stopped outside Clara's door.

'Should I knock?' he thought. Then he remembered that she didn't want any more adventures. He disappeared through the carriage door.

At that second, Clara put her head out of her room door. But she looked the other way, and didn't see the Doctor.

She left her room and knocked on his door.

'Doctor!' she called quietly through the door. 'Are you awake?' There was no answer.

'Too late,' she realised. 'He's gone to find the mummy!'

Further along the train, the Doctor was in a carriage full of machines and tools. Mrs Pitt's wheelchair from the dining room was in there. It was the one that she died in. But it was more than a wheelchair. It was also a high-tech computer. When a person sat in it, it checked their health. The doctor was very interested in it and he was testing it with his sonic screwdriver.

'It's a beautiful piece of equipment, isn't it, sir?' said a voice from the darkness. A man stepped forward. 'It's like a hospital on wheels,' the man continued. 'It keeps a person alive. It's very expensive, of course.'

'But it didn't help old Mrs Pitt, did it?' said the Doctor.

'You're right there, sir,' said the man. 'Perhaps it malfunctioned.'

'I don't think so,' said the Doctor, reading the information on his sonic screwdriver. 'The chair did everything possible to keep Mrs Pitt alive.'

'Yes, I know,' said the man. 'I checked it too.'

'Who *are* you? Why are *you* so interested in this chair?' asked the Doctor.

'Perkins, sir,' said the man. 'I'm the chief engineer on the Orient Express. And I don't like people dying on my train.'

'I'm the Doctor. And I like a good mystery. Pleased to meet you, Perkins.'

They shook hands.

'I've learned one thing from the chair, sir,' said Perkins. 'Mrs Pitt didn't die of old age.'

'Perkins, sir,' said the man. 'I'm the chief engineer on the Orient Express. And I don't like people dying on my train.'

The Killer in the Kitchen

Clara wanted to find the Doctor. He was doing something interesting without her. She got dressed again, and left her room. Suddenly, someone came through the door at the end of the carriage, walking fast. It was Maisie Pitt. She was wearing her night clothes and carrying a shoe. She pushed past Clara without seeing her.

'Hello?' said Clara.

Maisie didn't answer. She seemed frightened and worried.

'Are you OK?' asked Clara, calling after her. 'Excuse me!' she said more loudly, but the young woman didn't reply.

Clara followed her all the way to a door at the end of the train. The door had an electronic lock that was not from the year 1925.

'Excuse me,' said Clara again. She was behind the young woman now. 'It's Miss Pitt, isn't it? Are you all right? Can I do anything to help?'

The woman turned to Clara, still holding the shoe in her hand. It was pointing at Clara like a gun.

'My name's Maisie,' she said. 'And I'm not crazy.'

'I know you're not crazy,' said Clara kindly. 'You've just had a really bad day.'

Maisie turned back to the door.

'Computer!' she said. 'Open the door!'

The computer replied in a warm and friendly voice. Was it perhaps *too* friendly?

'Call me Gus,' it said. 'I'm afraid that only a train guard can open this door.'

Maisie tried pressing different numbers on the lock, but the door stayed shut. She was crying now.

'Are you OK?' asked Clara.

'They're refusing to show me her body,' said Maisie. 'I want to see her body. It's in this carriage.'

'I have a friend who's really good with locks,' said Clara. 'Let's go and find him.'

But Maisie wasn't listening. She turned back to the lock and hit it hard with her shoe.

The door opened immediately.

'Oh!' said Clara, surprised. 'Or you could use your shoe, of course. That works too!'

Clara followed Maisie into the dark carriage, and the door locked shut behind them.

The Doctor walked through the dining car. He was in a hurry and looking for someone. He stopped at a table where a man was sitting alone with a book and a cup of coffee.

'What's the most interesting thing about the Foretold?' the Doctor asked, pointing rudely at the man.

'I'm sorry,' said the man. 'I don't think we've met.'

He continued reading. The Doctor continued speaking.

'You know about the Foretold,' said the Doctor. 'It's a mummy. It's been around for thousands of years. There are many stories about it. "If you see it," says one story, "you're a dead man."'

'Yes, I know what the Foretold is,' said the man. 'You see, I'm ...'

'You're Professor Emile Moorehouse,' said the Doctor, finishing his sentence. The man looked surprised. 'You're Professor of Alien Science and History, and you know all the old stories. I'm the Doctor. Pleased to meet you.'

'Er ... yes,' said the professor. They shook hands.

'So, tell me the most interesting thing about the Foretold,' the Doctor repeated.

'Hm ... probably the sixty-six seconds,' said the professor. 'If the Foretold looks at you, you die exactly sixty-six seconds later. That's strange, I think.'

'No, no,' said the Doctor. 'That's not it. Try again.'

He took a silver cigarette case from his pocket and opened it. Inside were some brightly coloured sweets. He offered them to the professor.

Before the professor could answer, the Doctor continued. 'The Foretold first appeared in stories more than 5,000 years ago. Some stories say that it can be stopped with a secret word. Some people try to offer it money. Some people promise to live better lives. But nothing works.'

'You seem to know a lot about the mummy,' said the professor, eating a sweet.

'I read a lot of the old stories. Sometimes, parts of them are true.'

'Back on Earth, the old stories are dry and boring,' added the professor. 'They're always fiction. But here in space, everything is possible! The stories are more fun.'

The Doctor wanted to bring the conversation back to the Foretold. He guessed that they didn't have much time before the next attack.

'So, your ideas on the Foretold, Professor,' he said.

'Well, you can't run from it,' replied the professor.

'But you haven't noticed the most interesting thing, Professor,' said the Doctor. 'The most interesting thing is the fact that you are here. You know everything about the Foretold. The Foretold is here and you are here. Why is that?'

Suddenly the lights went dim. The clock started counting. ... 66 seconds ...

In the train's kitchen, the cooks were busy, preparing a meal for the passengers.

'What's that?' said Dumpy, one of the cooks, looking along the kitchen carriage.

'What's what, Dumpy?' asked another cook.

Dumpy was looking at the end of the kitchen carriage with wide eyes. He could see the mummy. It was looking back at him, and it reached a bandaged hand towards him.

... 56 seconds ...

'Can't you see him?' screamed Dumpy.

The mummy was moving towards him, between the ovens, passing the other cooks.

Dumpy picked up a large kitchen knife and waved it at the mummy. The other cooks laughed. They thought he was joking.

... 36 seconds ...

'There's nothing there, Dumpy,' one said.

'Calm down,' another said.

Dumpy stepped back again, not taking his eyes off the mummy.

'Get it away! Get it away!' he cried.

Then he was at the end of the kitchen. He threw down the knife and opened the door into the freezer room.

... 16 seconds ...

'Don't go in there!' shouted the other cooks. But Dumpy shut himself in the freezer. His frightened face appeared at the small window in the door. He was looking for the mummy. Where was it? Some of the other cooks were still laughing – surely it was a joke.

Then Dumpy turned around. The mummy appeared in the freezer with him. He screamed.

... 6 seconds ...

His back was against the wall now. Big pieces of frozen meat hung around him, but he didn't see them. The mummy was in front of him. Its ugly mouth was open and its hands were coming towards him. He felt them pressing on his head.

... zero ...

He fell to the floor of the freezer, dead.

'No!' shouted one of his friends. 'Dumpy! No!'

5

The Secret Shopper

'It was a heart attack,' said Captain Quell, looking at Dumpy's body. He was speaking to the other cooks. 'Do not say anything different to the passengers. If you do, you will lose your job on the Orient Express. Is that clear?'

'Yes, captain,' the cooks agreed.

The train's doctor completed his examination of the body. Then he closed Dumpy's body bag.

Clara was trying to open the electronic door from the inside. Mrs Pitt's body wasn't in fact in the end carriage and now the computer refused to open the door. It was dark in the carriage. Nothing happened when they tried the light switch.

'Perhaps I broke *all* the electronics with my shoe,' said Maisie, 'not just the door.'

Some light came in through the windows from suns far away, but Maisie wasn't interested in the view. She was clearly unhappy.

'Do you ever want bad things to happen to other people?' she asked.

'Oh, yeah,' said Clara. 'All the time. The person who built this door, for example.'

'She wasn't really my mother,' said Maisie, not listening to Clara's answer. 'She told me to call her "Mama". She was my grandmother. She wanted to keep her age secret.'

'You must really miss her.'

'You clearly never met her,' laughed Maisie. 'No, I just feel terrible because I've imagined her death so often. Did this happen because I wanted it to?'

'Hey, listen,' said Clara. She left the door and sat down next to Maisie. 'You didn't do anything wrong. Difficult people – well, they give you all kinds of thoughts. You didn't kill her. She just died.'

Then they saw something at the end of their carriage. It was a large box for the dead body of a tall human ... or a mummy. There was a small round window near the top of the box, like a large eye. Was the mummy inside? Clara stood up slowly ...

The Doctor followed Captain Quell and his guards along the train. He knew about the second death – the cook in the freezer – and he was angry with the captain. The captain wasn't taking the problem seriously enough.

'I think we need to talk,' he said to the captain.

'The passengers don't need to worry about this matter,' said Captain Quell, turning away. For him, the conversation was finished.

'I'm not a passenger,' said the Doctor.

'Who *are* you, then?' said the captain.

'I'm the worst thing you can think of,' said the Doctor. 'Who am I?' He took a card from his pocket and gave it to the captain. In fact, there was nothing printed on the card. But when people looked at it, they saw a name. They saw a name that frightened them.

'Oh no!' said the captain unhappily. 'A secret shopper!'

The Doctor looked surprised. Was a visit from a secret shopper really so bad? And weren't they called 'secret guests' when they secretly wrote reports on hotels, like this train, for the hotel company?

'OK,' he said, trying to act like a secret shopper. 'I was very cold in my room and I'm not pleased with the breakfast menu ...' The captain looked angrily at him. '... or the dying,' the Doctor added.

'Ssh!' said the captain. 'I don't want the other passengers to hear.'

He invited the Doctor to his office.

'Why aren't you doing something about these deaths?' asked the Doctor.

'They were accidents,' said the captain. 'We'll take the bodies off the train at the next stop. I've completed all the forms and spoken to the train's doctor. Everything's fine.'

'I'm sure it is,' said the Doctor. 'You've done enough – and no more. Your bosses will be pleased.'

'You don't know anything about me,' said the captain.

'I'm guessing that you were a soldier,' said the Doctor. 'You walk and talk like an officer.'

'I *was* an officer,' said the captain. 'I had a hundred men under me.'

'I'm sure you were an excellent officer,' said the Doctor. 'But you've seen terrible things, and you don't want to fight any more. You took this job for your last years of work because it was easy. Well, I'm sorry. This job stopped being easy when Mrs Pitt died.'

'Mrs Pitt had a heart attack ...' the captain started to say.

'Let's sit here and wait for the next "heart attack", shall we?' shouted the Doctor. 'Or, here's a crazy idea! We can do something to stop it!'

The captain looked very uncomfortable.

'Why am I even talking to you?' said the Doctor. He left the captain's office, shutting the door loudly behind him.

Chief Engineer Perkins was waiting for him. The engineer handed him the list of passengers, a plan of the train and the list of planet stops for the past six months.

'Quick work, Perkins,' said the Doctor. 'Perhaps it was too quick ...'

'Of course, sir,' said Perkins. 'I must be the mummy! Or perhaps I was already preparing this list for myself.'

They both smiled.

'Let's get to work,' said the Doctor.

'Who is this Doctor exactly?' asked Maisie. 'Is he your boyfriend?'

'No, we're not even friends. Not now,' said Clara.

'Well, that clearly isn't true,' replied Maisie. 'You're travelling together.'

'You're right.' Clara tried to explain. 'We've travelled around together … and now we're stopping. This is … er … I don't know, a goodbye to the good times.'

Maisie looked at the mummy-shaped box in the carriage. 'Were the good times all like this?' she asked.

'Yeah, they were,' Clara laughed.

'So why are you angry with him?' asked Maisie. 'Something has happened between you …'

'Well,' said Clara, 'it's a long story.'

'We've got plenty of time,' said Maisie.

So Clara told her about the baby alien on the Moon.

'And the doctor disappeared,' she said finally.

'He disappeared?' said Maisie. 'He left you alone to make the terrible decision?'

'I know!' replied Clara. 'What kind of friend does that?'

'What did you decide?' asked Maisie.

'I decided to save the baby alien,' said Clara. She finished the story. 'In fact, it was the right decision. The alien wasn't interested in the Earth. It flew away, and the Earth and the Moon were fine. But I was so angry with the Doctor. He left me there! Why didn't he help me to decide? When we met again he said, "It's *your* planet."!'

Death in the Bar

Back in the engineer's carriage, the Doctor, Perkins and Professor Moorehouse watched a video of Mrs Pitt's death from the camera in the dining car. The Doctor timed it.

'Sixty-six seconds exactly,' he said. 'The lights went dim. Did you notice?'

'Yes, the lights went dim in the kitchen too,' said Perkins. 'Just before the cook saw the mummy.'

'The old stories say that you can't kill the Foretold with a gun or a knife,' said the professor. 'It lives forever, you can't stop it and you can't kill it.'

'Now tell us the bad news,' said Perkins.

'So,' said Clara, finishing her story, 'I was alone on the Moon in an impossible position. And he put me there.'

'Oh, he was wrong,' said Maisie. 'He wasn't thinking about your feelings at all.'

'Exactly,' said Clara.

'And you got on a train with him ...'

'You can't end it with angry words,' said Clara. 'Not after so much time.'

Suddenly, they both jumped. Clara's phone was ringing.

It was the Doctor.

'Wake up,' he said. 'It's time for breakfast. And on this train, the breakfast ...'

'Doctor,' said Clara. 'Listen ...'

But he wasn't listening.

'... will taste wonderful!'

'Doctor,' repeated Clara. 'Please listen ...'

But he still wasn't listening.

'There's been another mummy murder,' he said. 'So our final trip is becoming more interesting.'

'The old stories say that you can't kill the Foretold with a gun or a knife,' said the professor. 'It lives forever, you can't stop it and you can't kill it.'

'Doctor,' shouted Clara. 'We're in the end carriage and we can't get out! I'm with Maisie Pitt!'

'What?' said the Doctor, listening now. He ran out of the engineer's carriage and along the train. He reached the end carriage door, with the phone still in his hand.

'Clara,' he called, knocking hard on the door. 'Are you in there?'

'Yes, we're here,' she said into the phone.

'Computer,' said the Doctor. 'Can you open the door, please?'

'Call me Gus,' said the computer. 'I'm afraid that only a train guard can open this door.'

The Doctor tried to open the door with his sonic screwdriver. It didn't work.

'Now the stupid sonic screwdriver isn't working,' said the Doctor on the phone to Clara.

'Why not?' asked Clara.

'I'm guessing that there's some kind of energy field around the lock. What are you *doing* in there? I thought you were asleep.'

'I was looking for *you*,' said Clara. '"There's nothing to worry about," you said. Yeah, right! Why didn't you knock on my door?'

'But you don't want any more adventures,' said the Doctor. 'You told me! Sometimes I think I'll never understand humans.'

Suddenly, something was happening in Clara's carriage. The tall, mummy-shaped box was beginning to open. Red light and smoke were pouring out.

'Doctor,' said Clara, 'I think your sonic screwdriver *is* working. It didn't open the door, but it did open a box in here ...'

'Is the mummy in there?'

'I think we're going to find out ... oh!'

'What is it?' shouted the Doctor.

'It's just ... it's empty!'

The lights went dim. The clock started counting. ... 66 seconds ...

'Clara!' shouted the Doctor. 'Did you see the lights go dim? The mummy's coming!'

Then a voice called behind the Doctor. 'Move away from the door!'

It was Captain Quell.

'My friend's inside, with Maisie Pitt.'

'Then they're in trouble too,' said Captain Quell. 'I spoke to my employers at Head Office. They didn't send a secret shopper to write a report on the train. You're not even on the passenger list.'

... 36 seconds ...

The captain called his guards forward. They pulled the Doctor away, along the train.

'How many people have to die, Captain,' called the Doctor, over his shoulder, 'before you start doing your job?'

At the same time, in the bar, one of the train guards was shooting his gun at an empty space. Then he shot at some glasses, and they broke into hundreds of pieces. The other passengers screamed and hid under the tables.

'Stay back!' cried the guard. 'Please don't hurt me!'

... 16 seconds ...

He fell to the floor while the mummy came closer. He shot again. The passengers screamed again.

Captain Quell ran into the bar. 'What do you think you're doing, man?' he shouted.

... 6 seconds ...

'Get up, man! That's an order!'

The guard was crying with fear. The black eyes and mouth of the mummy were above him. He put his arms up to try to protect himself.

'No, no!' he cried.

... zero ...

Those were his last words before he died.

The other guards now brought the Doctor into the bar.

'The answer is three,' said the captain. 'The answer to your earlier question. Three people have to die before I start doing my job, Doctor. You were right. I'm sorry I didn't listen to you.'

He told his guards to free the Doctor. The Doctor made a decision. It was time to speak to the passengers.

'Could you all listen to me, please?' he called. Everyone turned to him. 'There's an alien on this train. It chooses one victim at a time, and only the victim can see it. If you see it, you will die exactly sixty-six seconds later. But that isn't even the strangest thing on this train. Do you know what is?'

The passengers looked around, puzzled. Nobody answered.

'It's *you*,' he said, pointing at everyone in turn. 'You are from the best universities in the universe. You know more than anyone about aliens – the science, the history, the languages. Someone or something wants us to catch and understand this alien. And you are the best people for that job.'

'Who's chosen us?' asked Professor Moorehouse.

'I have no idea,' said the Doctor. 'But I think they're listening to us now.'

He smiled and looked up to the corners of the carriage.

'Where are you?' he shouted. 'Give us our orders!'

The Piece of Cloth

The train's engines stopped. The carriage doors locked shut. The Orient Express furniture disappeared. It wasn't 1925 now. Scientific equipment and hi-tech machines appeared on desks.

At the same time, some of the passengers disappeared.

'Where have they gone?' asked Perkins. 'Have they teleported?'

'They were never here,' the Doctor told him. 'They weren't real.'

A computer lit up.

'Good morning, everyone,' it said. It was Gus. As before, his voice was *too* friendly. 'Around the room you will find scientific equipment. We want to know what the Foretold is. We want to find its weakness and catch it. We want to understand how it works. We want to copy it. We want to make more mummies. And we want all of you to do the work for us. Isn't this exciting?'

'You don't know how to catch it?' asked the Doctor. 'So how did it get on the train?'

'A good question, Doctor,' said Gus. 'There is a very old piece of cloth on the wall at the end of the carriage. Look at it. It has strange shapes on it – perhaps a language that we don't know. You will always find the Foretold near this piece of cloth. *We* put the piece of cloth on the train.

The Foretold followed.'

The captain decided to act. He ran towards the piece of cloth, planning to throw it off the train. But he ran into a wall of energy around the cloth. He couldn't see the energy field, but he could feel it. It threw him back, and to the floor.

'And if we say no?' said Professor Moorehouse bravely to Gus. 'If we refuse to work, what will happen?'

'You can choose to do that, of course,' replied Gus. 'But the Foretold will simply kill you one by one.'

'How can we study something that we can't see?' asked the Doctor. 'What kind of alien is it? We have no idea!'

There was no time for Gus to answer. Suddenly, the lights went dim.

'Perkins,' shouted the Doctor. 'Start the clock.'

'It's about 1.8 metres tall, I think,' said Professor Moorehouse.

'Professor,' said the Doctor. 'You can see it!'

'Perkins,' shouted the Doctor. 'Start the clock.'

'I was looking forward to seeing a thousand-year-old alien,' said the professor. 'But now I'm not sure that I *want* to see it.'

'Bad luck,' said the Doctor. 'Tell us everything about it.'

'Fifty-six seconds,' said Perkins.

'Yes, of course,' the professor replied, putting on his glasses. He was sounding a little worried now. 'Er, well, it looks like a man in bandages.'

'What kind of bandages?' asked the Doctor. 'Old, new, clean, dirty?'

'Old, very old. They're falling off in places. I don't know what to tell you.' His voice was getting higher while the clock continued to count.

'Forty-six seconds,' said Perkins.

'Tell us something, man! You can see this thing,' the Doctor said. 'We can't. The smallest piece of information will help us save the next victim.'

'The next one?' said the professor. 'You mean I'm going to die? You mean you can't save me?'

'Well, no,' answered the Doctor. 'This *is* the end for you. But tell us more.'

'Er ... very old skin ... dry, hard. *Agh!*'

The mummy was reaching a hand towards the professor.

'Twenty-seven seconds,' said Perkins.

'Its back foot,' said the professor. He was speaking very fast. 'Er ... er ... it's pulling its back foot along the floor behind it. It seems to be hurt.'

'Tell us more!' the Doctor ordered.

'Leave me alone. I want to try and save my life,' said the professor. 'If you can say the right word, you can live!'

The professor's eyes were very wide.

'Those old stories won't help you now, Professor,' said the Doctor. 'This is real. Tell us what you can see!'

'Thirteen seconds,' said Perkins.

'This is *my* life,' cried the professor. '*My* death! I'm going to fight for myself.'

The professor spoke to the mummy. It was in front of him and he could smell it. 'I will give you everything I own,' he said, trying to defend himself with his arms.

The mummy put both hands around the professor's head and pressed hard.

'Zero,' said Perkins.

'The *Gloriana*, for example, was one spaceship. It spent three days trying to catch the Foretold. Every passenger was killed.'

Silence fell on the room.

'That was very unpleasant,' said a happy voice. It was Gus. 'And we are sorry. But it is not all bad news. You were able to study the professor's death closely. Well done, everyone!'

Perkins was looking at his computer. It was comparing information on the four deaths.

The Doctor gave white coats to everyone, and the scientists started work.

Then a phone rang and the Doctor answered it. It was Clara.

'We've found some papers in a box in the corner of this carriage, Doctor,' she said. 'They're passenger lists from other spaceships. Maisie knows some of the ships' names – they disappeared.'

Gus spoke again. His friendly voice was suddenly cold. 'Please end your telephone call and return to work,' he said.

The Doctor continued to talk to Clara.

'So we're not the first,' the Doctor said.

'No,' replied Clara. 'The *Gloriana*, for example, was one spaceship. It spent three days trying to catch the Foretold. Every passenger was killed.'

'Please end your telephone call and return to work,' repeated Gus. His voice was now very unfriendly.

'Then there was another ship …'

At the same time, in the kitchen car, the cooks were busy making sandwiches for the scientists. Suddenly, there was a loud noise and the kitchen computer began to give orders.

'Please leave the kitchen area,' it said. 'We are taking out the air from the kitchen area.'

The cooks were thrown around the carriage. All the ovens and equipment began to move towards the carriage doors.

A minute later, the scientists looked through the windows of their carriage and cried out. All the cooks and all their equipment were flying past, away into space.

'I think you should end your phone call, Doctor,' said Captain Quell quietly. 'He's punishing us – because you didn't listen to him.'

'I'm sorry,' said Gus. 'That was also unpleasant. But you must follow our orders. If you do not, I will take out the air from another area of the train. I will choose an area with less important passengers.'

Gus's words gave the Doctor an idea.

'Thanks for the help, Gus!' he said. He turned to the scientists. 'Gus is choosing passengers to kill. But how does the *Foretold* choose who to kill? I want a full history of each victim: their travels, their personal lives, their jobs – everything.'

'Please end your telephone call and return to work,' repeated Gus. His voice was now very unfriendly.

Sixty-six Seconds

The train wasn't flying now. Its engines were silent. It was simply hanging in space. The scientists continued to study the information.

'I can't find anything,' said Perkins. 'I've looked at their travel history, their interests, their health.'

'Their health!' said the Doctor. 'That's the answer. Mrs Pitt, the first victim, she was more than a hundred years old. She was the weakest passenger on the train.'

'But the cook was next,' said Perkins. 'He was young and healthy.'

Captain Quell was listening to their conversation.

'No, he wasn't,' he said. 'The cook *was* ill. He had bad stomach problems, but we kept quiet about it.'

'Because he worked with food,' said the Doctor. 'The next one – the guard?'

'He wasn't exactly ill,' explained the captain, 'but he was given a new heart two years ago.'

'And Professor Moorehouse,' said Perkins, checking his notes. 'He was in a car crash last year, and he's suffered terrible headaches since then.'

'So,' said the Doctor, 'it's choosing the weakest people first. It senses their illness. It may be a sickness of the body or the mind. But this is good news. We can guess who will be next.' Captain Quell was looking unhappy. 'I want the health records of everyone on this train. If anyone has had a cold, I want to know.'

The captain spoke quietly to the Doctor.

'You remember our earlier conversation?' he said. 'You were right. When I was a soldier, I saw terrible things. I fought in a war against the Daleks* on a planet far away from Earth. We were in an empty city because all the people were hiding in the mountains. The Daleks were moving through the city and shooting every living thing. I told my men to move into an old factory building. Then, before I could join them, a Dalek saw one of them through a window. My men were all killed – one hundred of them. And I was alive. I wasn't even hurt. Since then, I've had bad dreams every night. Sleep is almost impossible and, like Moorehouse, I get terrible headaches.'

'So you're probably next,' smiled the Doctor. 'That's good to know, Captain.'

'It's not good for *me*!' said Captain Quell.

'Well, of course,' said the Doctor. 'Not for *you*, because you're going to *die*. But for us, it will help us understand the Foretold.'

The captain looked at the Doctor. Where were this man's feelings? What kind of human was he? The captain didn't realise that he was talking to a Time Lord.

And then the lights went dim. Everyone in the carriage stopped working.

'Perkins,' said the Doctor, 'start the clock.'

He looked at the captain's face and he saw fear. The captain could see the Foretold. The scientists were ready with their notebooks.

'I can't see it clearly,' said the captain. 'It's like a bad dream. It gives me a headache just to look at it.'

He reached for his gun.

'No, no!' said the Doctor. 'That didn't work before.'

But the captain was a soldier. He didn't want to die without using his gun. He shot three times at the Foretold, but the Foretold didn't even notice the shots.

'Fifty seconds,' said Perkins.

*The Daleks: the Doctor's most dangerous enemies

But the captain was a soldier. He didn't want to die without using his gun.

'Where is it now?' asked the Doctor.

'It's about six metres in front of me and getting closer,' said the captain.

The Doctor ran to that place.

'Am I close?' he asked.

'Forty seconds,' said Perkins.

'Someone tell that man to be quiet!' shouted the captain.

'Am I close?' repeated the Doctor.

The mummy's hands were reaching through the Doctor's head; its fingers were coming through his eyes and mouth. The Doctor saw and felt nothing.

'It's passing right through you!' shouted the captain.

Perkins held up a scanner to the Doctor but the scanner couldn't see the Foretold.

'If you move, will it follow you?' asked the Doctor. 'Move back down the carriage, as quickly as you can.'

The mummy disappeared.

'It's teleported away,' said the captain.

Then the lights went dim again. The captain turned and saw the mummy. It was at the other end of the carriage now, and moving fast towards its victim.

'I think this is the end,' said the captain. 'It's not a bad way to go. I'm under attack and I'm looking the enemy in the face.'

He spoke his last words to the Doctor. 'Thank you for opening my eyes again, Doctor,' he said. 'We must always do what's right – to the end of our lives.' Then he cried out and fell to the floor.

'Zero,' said Perkins.

'It can teleport,' said the Doctor. He turned away from the captain's dead body and tried to understand the new information. 'The mummy uses a teleporter. And the sixty-six seconds. Why exactly sixty-six seconds? What takes sixty-six seconds?'

'A man has just died in front of us, Doctor,' said Perkins. 'Can we have a minute to remember him?'

'No, no,' said the Doctor. 'We can't do that. We can't think about the dead. We don't have time. We must think about the living.' He turned to the scientists. 'Everybody, what takes sixty-six seconds to change its state?'

There was silence.

'Why can't I see this thing?' he said. He walked up and down the carriage, throwing his hands in the air. 'I only need one minute with the mummy' he shouted, 'and this will end!'

'Doctor,' said Perkins. 'Are you really clever or do you just have a really high opinion of yourself? I'm not sure.'

'Both of those things are true,' said the Doctor. He continued to walk up and down, searching for ideas. 'This mummy has existed for hundreds of years,' he said. 'What keeps it alive? It's taking energy from living things … Perkins, pass me a scanner.'

He ran the scanner over the captain's dead body. It showed zero energy. But the Doctor was still puzzled by the sixty-six seconds.

'Why didn't the mummy just kill him? Why did it wait for more than a minute?'

'The mummy uses a teleporter. And the sixty-six seconds. Why exactly sixty-six seconds? What takes sixty-six seconds?'

'How long does energy take to move from one place in time and space to another?' asked Perkins. 'It's about a minute, isn't it?'

'Yes!' shouted the Doctor. 'Excellent! Well done, sir. That's why we can't see it. That's why we can't touch it. It's not in our time or space. This explains everything. Well, not everything. It doesn't explain what it is. It doesn't explain how it's doing it. But ... well done.'

'I think you should look at this Doctor,' said Perkins.

He pointed to his computer. It was clear who the mummy's next victim was.

The Soldier

'Maisie's had a bad day, that's all,' said Clara. She was on the phone to the Doctor, speaking quietly. She didn't want Maisie to hear.

'She's feeling unhappy and she's lost her grandmother,' the Doctor told her. 'She's the mummy's next victim. We've checked everyone's information on the computer. We're sure.'

Clara and Maisie were still in the carriage with the tall box. They still couldn't get out. Maybe that was a good thing.

'If we stay in here,' said Clara, 'the mummy can't get us.'

'It can appear in any part of the train, Clara,' said the Doctor, 'It can teleport. And we need her here. Even Gus the computer agrees with me.'

'OK,' replied Clara. 'And you can save her, right?'

'Of course not,' said the Doctor. 'But we can watch the mummy at work ...'

'... while it kills her.' Clara finished the Doctor's sentence.

'Yes,' said the Doctor, 'while it kills her. If it happens in *that* carriage, we won't be able to watch. Bring her to us.'

'*How* exactly?' asked Clara. 'She won't want to meet the mummy.'

'Well, I don't know,' said the Doctor. 'Lie to her. Tell her that, yes, I can save her.' He ended the call.

'What did he say?' asked Maisie, smiling at Clara.

Clara looked at Maisie. She didn't want to lie, but she had to. She knew that.

'He says that you're next. But he can save you,' she said.

Gus agreed with the Doctor that Maisie was probably the next victim. He opened the door to the carriage.

The two women ran out into the carriage where the suitcases were kept. The TARDIS was still parked there. Its lights came on when Clara appeared. It was like an old friend waiting for her.

'Why didn't I think of that?' Clara said to herself. 'The TARDIS can save Maisie.'

She ran towards the door, but something stopped her.

'What *is* that?' asked Maisie behind her.

'It's our time machine,' explained Clara. 'That's how we travel around the universe.'

'Of course,' said Maisie. 'And that's how the Doctor visited all those planets, like Thedium 4, thousands of years ago.'

'Yes,' said Clara. 'Before the Magellan Black Hole destroyed them. The TARDIS can take him anywhere at any time.'

'So he wasn't lying,' said Maisie thoughtfully.

'Let's take the TARDIS,' said Clara, 'and fly away. Then we can come back for the Doctor and the other passengers.'

Clara tried again to get into the TARDIS, but this time something pushed her back into Maisie. It was some kind of energy field.

'We'll go and see the Doctor,' said Clara. 'He'll be able to get into the TARDIS.'

They walked through the train to find the others. Gus opened the door for them into the carriage that was now full of scientists.

Clara told the Doctor about the TARDIS and the energy field.

'It's probably Gus,' said the Doctor. He was checking Maisie's energy with his sonic screwdriver while Maisie was smiling happily back at him. 'Gus doesn't want us to leave.'

Clara thought for a minute. A light went on inside her head.

'That's strange,' she said, looking closely at the Doctor. 'So he knows what the TARDIS is. That means ... He also knows who *you* are!'

'Well, he has invited me here before,' said the Doctor. 'He offered me free tickets, he sent a mysterious invitation ... He even phoned the TARDIS once!'

Clara hit the Doctor angrily with both her hands.

'"A quiet train journey through space," you said! You were lying! You *knew* this was dangerous.'

'I didn't *know*!' said the Doctor. 'I *hoped* it was.'

'This is why I'm leaving you,' Clara told him. 'You lied to me again. And now I've lied to Maisie, because of you!'

'What?' said Maisie. '*When* did you lie, Clara?'

'Maisie, I am so sorry,' Clara said.

At that second, the lights went dim. The mummy appeared ... and only Maisie could see it.

'Do I start the clock?' asked Perkins.

'Not yet,' said the Doctor. He held up the scanner in front of Maisie.

'Look at the scanner, not the mummy,' said the Doctor.

The scanner took away all Maisie's unhappy feelings from her mind. When the Doctor turned the scanner towards his own head, he fell back. Maisie's unhappiness filled his mind and he closed his eyes in pain.

'It's gone!' said Maisie. 'The mummy's gone! I can't see it.'

At that second, the lights went dim. The mummy appeared ... and only Maisie could see it.

'But *I* can,' said the Doctor. 'The mummy thinks that I'm you. So *I* can see it.'

He threw down the scanner and told Perkins to start the clock. The Doctor faced the Foretold.

'Hello,' he said. 'I'm pleased to meet you. I'm the Doctor and I will be your next victim this evening. But you can't hurt me for the next 53 seconds.'

... 52 seconds ...

'So,' the Doctor asked, 'how can I stop you? *Are* there secret words?'

He felt Maisie's feelings grow stronger inside him. He turned to her.

'You really didn't like your grandmother, did you?' he said. 'Your horse died when you were young. Do you remember that? It really *was* her. She killed it. Sorry.'

'Oh!' said Maisie, unhappy at the memory.

'And when your father died ... She killed him too.'

'No!' Maisie cried.

... 40 seconds ...

Now the Doctor looked more closely at the mummy. He noticed something. Under the bandages there were brown, green and black shapes – like the clothes that a soldier wears. He looked again at the piece of cloth on the wall. It too had strange shapes on it, like letters in an unknown language. And then he realised.

... 20 seconds ...

'Of course!' he said to the mummy, talking more and more quickly. 'It's not just a piece of cloth. It's a cloth on a stick – and you'll die for it. It's a flag! And if that's a flag, you're a soldier! You fought in a forgotten war thousands of years ago and you were hurt. The war ended but nobody told you. You want to die, but you can't. Why not? Because they changed you. They put a personal teleporter inside you, and lots of other equipment.'

... 10 seconds ...

'You can't stop killing until the war has ended...'

The mummy's hands reached out to the Doctor's head.

... 5, 4, 3, 2, 1 ...

'We surrender!' shouted the Doctor.

... zero ...

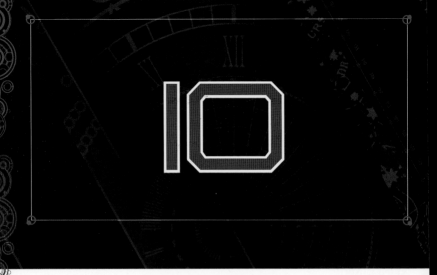

Ball of Fire

'I can see it again,' said Maisie.

They could all see it. The mummy was there, in the middle of the carriage. It dropped its arms and stepped back from the Doctor.

'Do I start the clock?' asked Perkins.

'No,' the Doctor told him. 'The clock has stopped.'

The Foretold stood up straight, facing the Doctor. It lifted its hand to its head, like a soldier.

The Doctor spoke to it. 'Your war has ended, soldier. You can stop fighting now.'

The Foretold fell to the floor and disappeared. There was nothing left except a pile of dirty bandages and a black box with red lights. The Doctor picked the box up.

'We were fighting *that*?' said Clara.

'The mummy was too,' he said.

'Listen,' said Clara. 'Remember what I said earlier ...'

'We haven't got time for that now,' said the Doctor quietly. 'We're not safe yet.'

He spoke loudly to the train's computer. At the same time, he waved his sonic screwdriver over the black box. He wanted to learn more about it.

'Well, Gus, we've solved your little puzzle. It was a five-thousand-year-old soldier with a piece of malfunctioning equipment inside him.'

'Thank you so much for your work,' said Gus. 'We are very grateful.'

'Who's "we"?' asked Clara quietly.

'No idea,' answered the Doctor.

Gus continued to speak. 'I am afraid that we do not need you now.'

'Oh!' said the Doctor. 'That's a surprise!' He wasn't really surprised, of course.

'I will now take out the air from *all* the carriages,' said Gus.

Almost immediately, most of the passengers put their hands to their chests and fell to their knees. The Doctor continued to work on the black box. The lights went dim and then went out. The only light now came through the window from passing stars.

'We hope you have enjoyed your journey on the Orient Express,' said Gus. 'Isn't it a wonderful train?'

'I imagine that you know a way out,' said Clara to the Doctor, speaking

The Foretold stood up straight, facing the Doctor. It lifted its hand to its head, like a soldier.

with great difficulty. The air was disappearing fast from the carriage.

'My enemy's enemy is my friend,' said the Doctor, '... when he has a personal teleporter.'

'Use it then,' said Clara urgently.

'It won't work,' said the Doctor. He was trying to mend the mummy's teleporter with his sonic screwdriver. 'I just need a few more minutes ... I'll tell you when I'm ready.'

'I'm not sure that we have a few more minutes ...' said Clara, and her eyes closed.

The Orient Express was falling slowly through space. Suddenly, there was a great crash, and the end carriage broke off in a ball of fire. Next went the carriage with the suitcases, then the bedrooms, then the dining car ... and finally, the bar. The fire burned and died. There was silence. There was no more Orient Express.

Suddenly, there was a great crash, and the end carriage broke off in a ball of fire.

The Beach

Clara opened her eyes. She was lying on a beach next to the sea. The TARDIS was a little further along the beach, and the Doctor was drawing in the sand with a stick. Not far away there were tall buildings, shiny and strange. A sun was shining, but it wasn't the Earth's sun.

'Ah, hello,' said the Doctor. 'Did you sleep well?'

'Weren't we on a train?' asked Clara, puzzled.

'Oh, that was hours ago,' said the Doctor.

'What happened?' asked Clara.

'We got off the train,' said the Doctor. 'The teleporter worked just in time. It took us all into the TARDIS. Then I tried getting into Gus's memory from the TARDIS. I wanted to know who Gus's friends were. He really didn't like that. So he destroyed the train … and perhaps himself.'

'Destroyed the train?'

'Yes, but we all got away. I gave everyone a lift to the nearest friendly planet.' The Doctor pointed to the shiny city.

'So you saved everyone,' said Clara. 'When I had to lie to Maisie …'

'I didn't want Gus to hear my plan and stop me.'

'So you really *do* have a heart,' said Clara.

'I have *two* hearts, as you know,' said the Doctor.

'And your plan worked,' said Clara.

'I wasn't sure. I couldn't save Quell,' said the Doctor. 'I couldn't save Moorehouse. Maisie was the lucky one. Sometimes you have to choose between two bad things, but you still have to choose.'

'You are a good man, Doctor,' said Clara. She thought about the time on the Moon when she had to choose between two bad results. Either she could save a baby alien or she could kill it. 'On the Moon,' she said, '*I* had to choose. You did the right thing. I understand that now.'

Perkins was the only passenger still in the TARDIS.

'Who or what was Gus, do you think?' he asked the Doctor.

'I'm not sure,' replied the Doctor.

'We never saw him, did we? Was he destroyed with the train?' asked Perkins.

'I don't think so,' said the Doctor. 'I think we may hear more from Gus in the future. He wasn't *really* interested in a mummy with a malfunctioning teleporter.'

The Doctor was getting ready to fly back to Earth. Perkins was very interested in how the TARDIS worked.

'I've never seen a TARDIS before,' he told the Doctor. 'It seems very clever. It was clearly built by a Time Lord. But I notice that it needs some work. It makes a terrible noise when it lands. You need someone to check it for you.'

The Doctor liked Perkins. He was clearly an excellent engineer, and very calm when things were going badly. He had good ideas. He understood how things worked. They made a good team.

'Chief engineer of the TARDIS. How does that sound to you?' asked the Doctor. 'You can travel with me for a year or two.'

'I don't think so,' said Perkins. 'I don't need that much excitement in my life. The Orient Express was my last job. It's time to hang up my tools. I want to enjoy my old age.'

They shook hands and said goodbye, and Perkins left the TARDIS.

'Do you love it?' Clara asked the Doctor.

'Love what?'

'Do you love making really difficult decisions?'

'Why do you think that I love that?' asked the Doctor.

He continued to prepare the TARDIS.

'Because it's your job,' said Clara. 'All day, every day. That's what you do.'

'It's my life,' said the Doctor, puzzled.

'It doesn't *have* to be,' said Clara. 'Your planet, Gallifrey, is out there. Why don't you live there for the rest of your life?'

'Gallifrey is lost,' said the Doctor. 'I can't find it.'

'Well, stay on Earth,' said Clara. 'You seem to like being with us humans.'

'I don't think so,' said the Doctor.

'Do you *need* to do it?' asked Clara. 'Are you lost without the dangerous adventures and hard decisions?'

'How do I know,' said the Doctor, 'if I don't try?'

'Will you *ever* try?' asked Clara.

'Stop asking me, Clara,' said the Doctor. He never enjoyed talking about why he did things.

Suddenly Clara's phone rang. The Doctor knew it was Danny. He turned away. He felt sad that this was Clara's last adventure. He also knew that Danny was good for her.

Clara ran to a quieter part of the TARDIS.

'Hey, Danny!' she said. 'How are you?'

'I'm fine,' he said. 'Has the journey finished?'

'Yeah,' said Clara. 'The Doctor has saved the world again. I can't talk now, but I'll see you soon. And ... um ... I love you.'

'I love you too,' said Danny.

'Hah!' Clara laughed. 'I can't imagine why!'

She pressed 'End Call' on her phone. Then she stood for a minute, lost in thought. She made a decision.

'Was that Danny?' called the Doctor. 'What did he want?'

'He's fine with it,'

'Sorry, what …?'

'Danny. He's fine with it. With the idea of you and me travelling together. Flying around the universe.'

'Wasn't it his idea that we should stop?' asked the Doctor.

'Yes, but he's decided that he doesn't mind. And *I* don't! So that wasn't our last journey. Let's have more adventures …'

The Doctor was surprised, but pleased.

'That's a big change,' he said happily.

They both had big smiles on their faces.

'Yes,' said Clara. 'Changes happen. Listen,' she explained. 'If I get home safely and on time after each trip, everything is great. I'm so sorry. I thought that we were finished. But we're not. We're fine. So take me to some new planets!'

'Well, I'm very glad to hear that,' he said. 'I know a wonderful planet where everyone's happy all the time … Are you sure about this?'

'Are *you*?' said Clara. 'Have you *ever* been sure?'

'No,' said the Doctor.

'Then what are we waiting for?' said Clara. 'Let's go.'

Noises came from the TARDIS. Then it disappeared.

Activities

Chapter 1

Before you read

1 Discuss these questions.

    a Have you ever watched *Doctor Who* on TV? What do you know about the show?

    b Do you think we will find life on other planets in the next fifty years? How?

2 Look at the Word List at the back of the book. Find a word:

    a for something that you can wave in a crowd.

    b for something that you can tie around a broken arm.

    c for something that you walk through at an airport.

3 Now read *In this story* and the *Introduction* at the beginning of this book. Which of these facts about the Doctor are true (✔)?

    a The Doctor is human.

    b He has two hearts.

    c He is always shooting people dead.

    d His body is 2,000 years old.

    e His spaceship is bigger on the outside than the inside.

    f He usually travels with a human companion.

    g The Doctor has been on TV since 1963.

    h Eleven different actors have played the Doctor.

While you read

4 Circle the correct words in *italics*.

    a The Orient Express is travelling to *Istanbul / different planets*.

    b This story takes place *in 1925 / in the future*.

    c *An old lady / A young woman* can see a man dressed as a mummy.

    d The head waiter *can / can't* see a mummy.

    e Maisie thinks that the old woman is *ill / crazy*.

f The Doctor and Clara join the Orient Express *in the TARDIS / at a planet stop.*

g *The Doctor / Danny* is Clara's boyfriend.

h Clara is *angry / happy* with the Doctor.

After you read

5 Discuss these questions.

   a How do we know that things are not right between Clara and the Doctor?

   b Imagine that a mummy walks into your classroom. Only you can see it. How do you feel? What do you do?

   c What is the most exciting train journey that you have been on?

Chapters 2-3

Before you read

6 Discuss these questions. What do you think?

   a Chapter 2 is called 'The Sad Smile'. Who will have a sad smile?

   b Who or what is the mummy?

   c Will the mummy kill again?

While you read

7 Who is speaking? Write the name.

   a 'It's a smile, but you're sad.' ....

   b 'Isn't it beautiful?' ....

   c 'I really thought that I hated you.' ....

   d 'Kill it!' ....

   e 'That's a lie.' ....

   f 'Perhaps Miss Pitt was right about you.' ....

8 Put these words in the right sentences.

alive	dangerous	excited	happy	interested
natural	unusual	worried		

a The Doctor thinks that there is nothing .... about the death of the old lady.

b Clara isn't .... about ending her travels with the Doctor.

c Danny isn't .... about this trip on the train.

d Clara doesn't think that this trip is ....

e The Doctor is .... about the mystery of the mummy.

f The Doctor is .... in Mrs Pitt's hi-tech wheelchair.

g The chair tried to keep Mrs Pitt ....

h Perkins doesn't think that Mrs Pitt's death was ....

After you read

9 Imagine that you are Clara and you are on the Moon. You have to decide:

a Do we kill the alien baby?

b Do we let the alien baby live?

Which will you choose? Which did Clara choose, do you think?

Chapter 4

Before you read

10 Discuss these questions.

a How does Perkins think that Mrs Pitt died? Write down three ideas. (Remember that only Mrs Pitt saw the mummy.)

b This chapter is called 'The Killer in the Kitchen'. Who do you think the killer will be?

While you read

11 Circle the mistakes in these sentences. Write corrections.

a Maisie Pitt stops to speak to Clara.   ....

b She's carrying a gun.   ....

c Clara says that she is crazy.   ....

d The train's computer is called Maisie.   ....

e Clara wants to see Mrs Pitt's body.   ....

f Maisie locks the door with her shoe.   ....

12 You are a passenger on the Orient Express. Complete this information about the mummy for the University of Alien Studies.

Name: The ....
Alien ⬡   Human ⬡
Age: ....
Time between someone seeing the mummy and dying:

....

Ways to stop the mummy that don't work:
Say a .... word.
Offer it ....
.... to live a better life.
.... away.
Person who knows most about it: ....

After you read
....

13 Work in groups of five. One of you is Dumpy, one of you is the mummy, two are the cooks, and one is the speaking clock. Act out the killing of Dumpy.

Chapters 5-6

Before you read
....

14 Discuss why the mummy has chosen – from all the possible passengers – old Mrs Pitt and a cook in the kitchen. Note down your ideas.

While you read
....

15 Are these sentences right (✔) or wrong (✘)?

a The Doctor checks the cook's body.
b Mrs Pitt was Maisie's grandmother.
c The captain is very worried about the killer.
d The Doctor's card says 'secret shopper'.
e The captain hates secret shoppers.
f The Doctor wants to stop more killings.

g Maisie can see that the Doctor is very important to Clara.
h The sonic screwdriver opens the train doors.
i The mummy-shaped box is empty.
j The captain's employers knew about the Doctor.
k The Doctor tells the passengers that there is an alien on the train.

After you read

16 Look back at your answers to Activity 9. Were you right? Did you and Clara make the same decision?

17 Work in pairs and have this conversation.

Student A: You are the Doctor. You are very angry with the captain. You think that he isn't doing his job.

Student B: You are Captain Quell. You have just realised that these deaths are serious. Explain to the Doctor that you were wrong. Say that you are sorry.

Chapter 7

Before you read

18 'There's an alien on this train. ... If you see it, you will die exactly sixty-six seconds later. But that isn't even the strangest thing on this train.' What *is* the strangest thing, and how can you explain it?

While you read

19 Number these sentences in the correct order, from 1 to 9.

a Captain Quell tries to throw the piece of cloth off the train.
b Clara and the Doctor speak on the phone.
c Gus kills everyone in the kitchen car.
d Professor Moorehouse sees the mummy.
e Scientific equipment appears in the dining car.
f Some of the passengers disappear.

g The Doctor says he can't save the professor.
h The lights go dim and the clock starts.
i The mummy presses its hands on the professor's head.

After you read

20 Work in pairs and have this conversation.

Student A: You are a reporter for The Universe Times. You have heard that there is a mummy on the Orient Express. Phone the train and ask a scientist about it.

Student B: You are a scientist on the Orient Express. Answer the reporter's questions. Give the reporter all the information that you have after Professor Moorehouse's death.

Chapter 8

Before you read

21 The next victim dies in Chapter 8. Who will it be, do you think?

While you read

22 The mummy has now killed five people on the train. Match the each name to the reason they died.

a Mrs Pitt	i) headaches
b Dumpy	ii) a new heart
c the train guard	iii) old age
d Professor Moorehouse	iv) bad dreams
e Captain Quell	v) stomach problems

After you read

23 Look back at your answer to Activity 21. Were you right?

24 The Doctor couldn't save the professor or the captain. How does he feel about that, do you think? Give reasons for your answer.

Chapters 9-10

Before you read

25 The Doctor and Perkins know who the next victim will be. Who do you think it will be? Why?

While you read

26 Are these sentences right (✔) or wrong (✘)?

a Clara and Maisie will be safe if they stay in the end carriage.

b The Doctor says he can save Maisie.

c The TARDIS can save Maisie.

d Gus has put an energy field around the TARDIS.

e The Doctor isn't surprised about the trouble on the Orient Express.

f He can see the mummy when it first appears.

g He takes Maisie's feelings and memories into himself.

h The Doctor realises that the mummy is a soldier.

i He tells the mummy that the war has ended.

j The mummy doesn't believe him and tries to kill him.

k The Doctor knows who Gus works for.

l The Doctor tries to mend the personal teleporter.

After you read

27 What lie did Clara tell Maisie? Is it acceptable to lie to people sometimes? When? Give some examples.

Chapter 11

Before you read

28 Discuss these questions.

a The Orient Express is a ball of fire. Has the Doctor saved everyone, do you think? If he has, how?

b Clara is going to make a big decision in the final chapter. What will it be?

While you read

29 Write answers to these questions.

a Where does Clara wake up?

....

b What and who saved everyone? (List three people or things.)

....

c Why did the Doctor lie to Clara about Maisie?

....

d Who does the Doctor offer a job to?

....

e Why doesn't the Doctor go back to Gallifrey to live?

....

f Does the Doctor want Clara to leave Danny?

....

g Does Danny tell Clara that he is happy for her to travel with the Doctor?

....

h How does the Doctor feel about Clara's change of plan?

....

After you read

30 Discuss these questions.

a Why does Clara decide to continue travelling with the Doctor?

b What will Danny say when he hears the news?

c Has Clara made the right decision? What do you think?

Writing

31 Imagine that you meet an alien. The alien seems friendly. What questions will you ask it? Write a list of twenty.

32 You are in the TARDIS with Clara and the Doctor. You can choose to go anywhere in time and space. Choose a year. Choose a place. Explain your reasons.

33 Many people are needed to work on the Orient Express in space. The train has a captain, guards, a head waiter, cooks, an engineer, a doctor. Choose one of the jobs. Describe a day's work on the King of Trains.

34 Choose one of the pictures in the book. Write a description of it: Who is in it? What is happening? What has just happened? What is going to happen next?

35 Clara arrives back on Earth. She meets Danny and they talk about Clara's mummy adventure. Danny asks questions and Clara answers them. Write their conversation.

36 Imagine Clara stops travelling with the Doctor. The Doctor needs a new companion. Write a job description. Use this title: *Companion Wanted!*

37 You work at the BBC and you are going to show a group of people around the TARDIS. What will you tell them? Write your talk.

38 You are the Doctor. Write to a friend from another planet. Your friend has never met a human. Tell your friend what humans are like.

Word List

alien (n) a fictional being from another world.

bandage (n/v) a long, narrow white cloth that is tied around a broken arm, for example.

captain (n) the officer who gives the orders on a ship or a spaceship, for example.

carriage (n) one of the parts of a train that carry passengers; some carriages are also called **cars**.

dim (adj) **go dim** to become less bright.

energy (n) something that makes movement possible. Energy can come from the sun, for example. Food gives us energy.

engine (n) the machine that drives a car or train; an engineer is someone who looks after engines.

flag (n) a piece of cloth, often tied to a stick. Each country has a national flag with its colours on.

human (n/adj) a person from Earth.

malfunction (v) to fail to work correctly.

mummy (n) a dead body protected by oils and bandages.

planet (n) something, like Earth, Mars and Jupiter, that moves around a star through space.

professor (n) a teacher with an important position at a university.

puzzle (n) something that is difficult to explain or solve. If you are **puzzled** by something, you don't understand it.

scanner (n) a piece of equipment that you pass over something or someone in search of full information.

surrender (v) to stop fighting because you cannot win.

technology (n) modern machines and equipment that come from scientific ideas. **Hi-tech** machines use the most recent technology.

teleport (v) to disappear from one place and appear in another, using your mind or special **technology**. A **teleporter** is an imaginary machine in which you can travel very, very fast.

universe (n) all of space and time and everything in it.

victim (n) someone who is killed or hurt.